Good Thunder, Blue Earth

"Good Thunder and Blue Earth are places in southern Minnesota, though the terms, 'southern' and 'Minnesota,' don't seem to go together. But like the title, these different voices hold together with familial ties and a sense of belonging to the land and tradition.

This book is a family saga told by ten characters. Some 'walk the beans checking damage from ice balls.' Others find delight in 'counting snowflakes pulsing under yard lights.' The voices are clearly delineated as they take turns speaking of their own concerns and their relationships with the other characters.

GOOD THUNDER, BLUE EARTH is written from a rich tradition of personal narratives, reminiscent of the SPOON RIVER collection. Susan Stevens Chambers picks up the nuances of weather, of speech, and of people familiar with the land and each other. Reading these poems, I also felt that the land was a character with its tenants of bean pods, corn, peas, cannas and soy bean. I'm glad Chambers has preserved these narratives in their time and place.

There is a strong lyricism in these narratives. They are full of insights and values of basic Americana. GOOD THUNDER, BLUE EARTH is an amazing harvest of sound and image. It is a fine volume of poetic monologues that create a landscape of unified stories of human endurance."

Diane Glancy

*To Liz —
as you wed —
who understands
the importance of
family! Aunt Sue*

GOOD THUNDER, BLUE EARTH

Poems of the farmland and its people

Susan Stevens Chambers

SUSAN STEVENS CHAMBERS

417 North First Street
Brainerd, MN 56401

218.851.4843

www.riverplacepress.com

Copyright 2016, RiverPlace Communication Arts, LLC

No part of this book may be reproduced or transmitted in any form or by any means—graphic, electronic, or mechanical, including photocopying, recording, or any information storage or retrieval system—without written permission from the publisher, except for brief quotations included in a review.

First Edition

ISBN Number: 978-0-9903563-6-3

DEDICATION

To Wayne Knewtson, for his farming expertise

To John Rezmerski, for his poetry proficiency,

and to the farmers of Southern Minnesota,
who helped me really taste the land

CAST OF CHARACTERS 8

GOOD THUNDER, BLUE EARTH 9

ACT ONE: THE CARLSON'S CENTURY FARM

Breathing In (Jo) 11
Cage From Within (Grandma Mildred) 12
Biding Time (Grandpa Hank) 13
Bill The Farm Hand (Bill) 14
Loving In Planting Season (Jo) 15
When Things Are Good (Jake) 16
Morning at the Courthouse (Grandpa Hank) 17
Next Year For Me (Lynnette) 18
Head To The Clouds (Kyle) 19
Hayloft's Gift of Night (Jake) 20
Windshield Window Peeping (Jake) 21
Behind The Barn On Graduation Day (Grandpa H) 22
Kyle Graduates (Jo) 23
John Deere $93,000.00 Sale (Mabel Prangle) 25
Still ahead: The Rest of July and All of August 26
Gambling With July (Jo and Jake) 27
Preserving The Moment 28
The Way of Crickets 29

Act Two: Turns

Watching the Nest (Jo) 31
I Do Not Mind (Kyle) 33
Family Farm Changes (Jake) 34
On The Verge (Jo) 35
Planting Time (Jake) 36
The Rise and Fall (Grandma Mildred) 37
Northern Comfort (Asa Prangle) 38
The Race (Lynnette) 39
To Take to Heart (Grandpa Hank) 40
Down The Hall (Jo) 41
In The Room (Jake) 42
The Doctor's Prescription 43

Act Three: Harvest

Nearing Culmination (Jake) 45
The Product of Labor (Jake and Lynnette) 46
Predawn Ritual (Jo) 47
Full Circle (Jo) 48
Aftermath of Corn Harvest (Jo) 50
Finishing Touches (Jake) 51
Vacation From Ag. School (Lynnette) 52
A Low Oklahoma Hooker (Grandma Mildred) 53
After The Blizzard (Bill) 55
Staving Off Ghosts (Jo) 56
Making Do (Jake) 57
January Progress (Jake) 58

Acknowledgements 59
About the Author 60

CAST OF CHARACTERS

Jake Carlson
Jo Carlson

Grandpa Hank Carlson
Grandma Mildred Carlson

Lynnette Carlson
Kyle Carlson

Bill the Farm Hand

Arnold Brocker

Asa Prangle
Mabel Prangle

Good Thunder, Blue Earth

They are fighting again,
snapped by July days that scream summer,
overwhelmed by one too many "making do's".

Their voices are tight with pain and differences,
they cannot find common ground.
Uncomfortable
when their parents sound like them,
the kids slink to another room.

In the kitchen, discontent rumbles,
builds
    higher and higher
        until it roils white and gray,
            flashes out.
First one strike,
        two
a cloudburst of stress:
the room fills,
        fills.

Then it is done.

Throats hoarse, the words flap tiredly.
They stare across coffee cups and hear
together the good thunder,
low and singing from the west.

Rising like swallows from a line,
they stand on the porch in wind gone cool.
The cloudbank turns day to night,
brings the rain.
Drops hit rich dirt, soak the soil,
gives them a harvest.
The earth turns deep blue, growing.

When the kids come to the porch
they see their parents kiss.
In time thunder and rain roll off.
The yard drips clean.
A new moon dodges cloud wisps
above their field.

Good Thunder, Blue Earth

Act One: The Carlson's Century Farm

BREATHING IN (Jo)

Hear the song of melt.
Our field sunrises up,
sheds snow.
Water races in the ditches.
Our acres stir in the change.

I watch Jake's eyes.
For months he has woven
frigid dreams, stuck at the computer.
He booked appointments with the banker,
actually kept them,
taking in the neat configurations
that mean the farms will live another year.

He goes to his parents' farm
to check and see if maybe a mile further
down the road it is closer to spring.
Then he comes home and stares
across the bean field.

It is too soon to think about planting.
The furrows hold ice.
He is like our cat, at the door one minute,
bearing the bitter wind
so he can smell the going of snow.

He can't walk the fields:
they suction against anyone
foolish enough to try.
But he stands at the edge.
He bends down, placing a finger
in the soil, and licks.
His face thrusts forward, tasting the air.
The cat rubs against me,
yowls,
wanting to go out again.

CAGE FROM WITHIN (Grandma Mildred)

I have spent my life
looking into the yard
through screen patterns,
like our lop-eared rabbit
tucked in her hutch
who eyes the dog—safe, but cautious.
This screen door pulls the day into my kitchen,
warns of intruders.
Lord, many a noon dinner I have spent
back against my screen,
summer wind on my wet neck,
while a dozen men move like hailstorms
through piles of muffins, chicken,
potatoes and pie
baked when screen wires
glowed red with sunrise.

The screen dapples my view of the yard,
lines crossed over the men shoveling grain.
From behind here I watch my Hank
broil like a thunderstorm
because he cannot face his age.
I watched Jake pick a woman
who never gave the farm the things I did.
I watch his children repeat
all the tricks of their father.

Patterns of screen
mottle my skin.
They are now a part of me,
river over the back of my hands,
crisscross my eyes,
line my cheeks.
I have hidden here by my door
for so long I am no longer secure
without the screen's cool protection
in front of me.

ACT ONE: THE CARLSON'S CENTURY FARM

BIDING TIME (Grandpa Hank)

I scuff across the yard where Jake,
back bent over the planter,
is doing it all wrong.
I hand him the wrench.
He could have been in the fields
half an hour ago if only he would listen
to my warnings.
I start again to tell him that,
stop when I see his face.
He wipes the sweat from his eyes,
asks me if I can lift seed into the planter.
I hate it when he calls me "Pop".

These bags get heavier each year.
It seems my back tricks me.
Bill, the hand, reaches over,
hefts up the sack.
When I was their age
I worked 600 acres by myself.
Bill mounts the tank truck,
rumbles off.
Jake wipes his hands,
leaps up on the machine with a shout.

I am left alone to clean up the tools.
Mildred, shaded by the screen door,
shakes her head, gives me a Jake-look.
Finally she says what has been
beside us all week:
   "You are too hard on the boy.
    Let him run the place.
    We ought to move to town."

"NO!"
I know how the town claws into you.
The only way you get back to the land
after the town gets you is in a long black car,
in front of a row of cars, headlights on,
aimed for the hilltop cemetery.

She sighs in frustration, moves from the doorway.
   "Come to supper, now. And Grandpa,
    you have dirt under your nails."

BILL THE FARM HAND

When grandfather ventured from his fjords
luck tossed him to the north side of this state.
He chose a claim there although settlers
spoke of richer soils south. He and Pa attacked the land:
struck trees, hefted rocks. Our neighbor Sven took one look
at the size of them, cussed the glaciers, and turned
out dairy cows to shadow between trees.

Pa and Grandfather laughed at him.

They marked their days off with sweat, heaving boulders,
with a growing pain running down their spines.
Each time they opened a field it grew more rocks.
It killed grandfather, finally. He staggered in the flax—
heart turned granite—fell and rolled into the rock pile.

Sven prospered.

My father bent over those stones. He cursed,
watched meager grain shrivel in the sand.
One day they were too big.
He walked away from the farm
  the mortgage,
    the other kids and me,
      he walked away from Ma.

She said I would slip off, too.
When she lost the farm I tried to stay,
but I hated the place in town. I drifted south,
avoiding cities. I searched for stoneless living.

So I came to the Carlsons.
This county tastes of black soil:
I work the entire field and never turn a rock.
The Carlsons are good people. But sometimes, while
perched high on the bins working the corn downward
like Sven's daughter shaking out her hair,
I wonder if the Carlsons know
that their prosperity rests so much
on stones,
      rain,
          luck and the choices
              their grandfather made.

LOVE IN PLANTING SEASON (Jo)

Some spring mornings I would gladly
throw my paycheck away just
to have a day in the garden
digging in cannas, hoeing peas.
But my outside job keeps Jake
one step ahead of the bank,
free to stay on the farm.

Freedom. Such freedom!
Jake will never go on vacation;
no time for theater or to watch
Kyle hit his first homerun;
hear Lynette play her piano solo.
I could do without such freedom.

Mother Carlson and I
don't see eye-to-eye on much,
but she warned me of hours spent
at the door on harvest nights
watching headlights move the corn rows,
never knowing when they will come back.

She knows of Mother's Day—
placed in the middle of planting
season by the devil himself.

She knows of reaching in a warm bed
in pre-light autumn hours,
finding only the hollow where he was.
She knows how our needs
will always come after the farm.

WHEN THINGS ARE GOOD (Jake)

The mist—fine as my first tiny soy beans
peeping up in thin rows—
softens the woods near the field.
It makes me sing. I go low and deep
as I feed the cattle.
                                  They are not impressed.
All around the wet smells strong.
As I cross the yard it soaks my face.
During planting I was glad enough for sun
but as I rode the tractor I felt the dust
spiral up and rush away from the wheels.
I tried to ignore it,
        tried not to notice nine more days of sun
        after we finished the planting.

But now there is rain.
Pop grumbles about his arthritis,
but as the mist turns to heavy drops
on our backs he laughs,
tells me tall tales.

Today I enjoy hearing them.
Oh, sometimes we spark and I burn against his words:
        when I cannot do anything
            the way he thinks it must be done,
when he will not let go,
until I want to throw my tools down
and stomp off to some office job.

But not today.
Not tomorrow, either, and we both know it.

We stand, letting the water pour over us,
we watch our new green corn and inhale.

MORNING AT THE COURTHOUSE (Grandpa Hank)

The parking lot full.
On the first floor reporters jam near
the county commissioners spank-new offices.
I stop there for a bit and take a chaw.
The reporter hits Commissioner Bunde pretty hard
about money wasted on the dam project.
I snort.

The elevator up to second floor
shakes more than Arnold's old tractor.
Hallway there is crammed.
Deputy Keller is jawing with
a spiffed-up young guy in a blue suit.
Saw a lady lawyer—slender, intense
dressed in a spotless cream colored jacket.
I just don't know about these gals.
Bailiff comes by, asks me if I am a juror?

"No, came to pay my taxes."

Back to that elevator.
This level is duller, hallway empty.
All the clerks huddle back in a corner.
They break out in giggles.

I clear my throat—one, two times.
No one looks up.   Finally I spit.
That gets them, one saunters over.
She takes the farm account check;
six thousand dollars for 800 acres,
two times a year.
She stamps the bill, pops her gum,
and turns away without a word.
I shrug my shoulders.

Court is in session back on second floor,
so I slip in. The white haired judge with bushy eyebrows,
sounds like a judge should. The drunk hangs his head.
I sit until nearly dinner time, then hurry back to the farm.

Jake wanted to mail the taxes in—
without this trip
my May and October
would be just like any other months.

NEXT YEAR FOR ME (Lynnette)

The heat wavers in front of me but
the opened earth smells cool below my machine.

Kyle let me do his job again—
his grin flashed when I suggested it—
as quick as the scowl I saw flicker over him
when Dad said he had to work the west forty.

Now he is immersed with his planes,
no downward glance for me or this field.
It suits us both. He loves the air.
I love to drive here,
sink blades deep into the land.

Dad still calls me "Baby".
His face will be black as this dirt
when I jiggle back to the yard.
He can't see me when he is
so angry at Kyle.
I wish my cultivator work
made him smile like he did
when I wore my green dress
to junior prom.

Mom loves city lights,
seems to float above this land
as if she didn't feel the warmth.
How will she understand when I reject
the university next year, go to agriculture school?

Each year Dad tells Kyle to look sharp so
he will know how to manage the place some day.

Kyle! Who dreams only of reaching blue sky;
who runs away on wings.

Dad waves his wrench at Kyle,
shouts about the untouched hay.
I stand behind them, silent.
Alfalfa wafts warm
from the nearby pasture
and I want,
      I want,
           I want to farm so hard.

HEAD TO THE CLOUDS (Kyle)

When I was ten Dad let me ride
with the crop-duster pilot.
Each time we rolled up over
the field edge and screamed
into the clouds I laughed.

I wish I could explain to them:
how the high air is cleaner than spring;
how the land below reveals logic
you miss from the ground.

Lynnette tries to understand,
just as I try to care about
the acres she bubbles on about.
But our small patch of land—
only a corner of the pattern—
is not enough for me.

Dad chose his life.
He smiles as he feeds cattle,
always whistles in the yard.
Mom hums to herself
as she puts on her suit,
has time apart from the farm.

It's my turn.

Mom knows. She chuckles over my flying stories,
but I see her eyes. They flicker fear.
I don't care. I am not afraid.
I want my shadow to pass over the earth.
I love the speed,
    the crazy speed;
        I want to roar up
            every day, free.

HAYLOFT'S GIFT OF NIGHT (Jake)

The barn is dark. The persistent
south wind is muffled in here.

Above me dots of bright
sparkle;
they are escapees from small holes
in the wall.
I reach, tap dust motes.
They climb the shafts of light
two stories up.

The barn is night folded into itself,
ignoring the heat outside.

Today has been kind:
at sunrise a warm blue mist
rolled through the corn,
filled the bean pods.
Now it's late afternoon.
Although there are no clouds,
the moist winds sing of rain.

In the quiet of this tall room
I feel the sun beyond.
It wraps below the stalks
in my field, boosts the corn higher.

I listen to the horse,
museum hushed,
breathe in, out.

High overhead the old plank wall
is ladened with chinks.
They turn the loft into a midnight pasture
full of fireflies.
Here where day is night
they are a silent celebration,
festive until the sun beyond
blinks out and takes
this inner night away.

WINDSHIELD WINDOW PEEPING (Jake)

Arnold Brocker is walking the beans.
He is an old barn:
    colors cold as dusk,
        walls and roof precarious.

He comes to tread the rows
dressed in striped coveralls,
long sleeves,
his stained DeKalb hat perched like
a rusty cupola on his head.

He starts at noon when the temperature
is already ninety and thunderheads
hint in the piercing blue.
He moves the rows slowly,
like his rattling tractor.

His ancient smoker is a midget
compared to the new John Deere's.
It was nearly ten years ago
that bean riders waved back at him,
sprayers held firmly away from bare legs.
No one else rides—or walks—beans these days.

Along the line where the field becomes woods
stands an elm, eighty years tall.
It withers this summer.
Blighted leaves release with each breeze.
Those who rush the road
look past Arnold's stooped shoulders
at the gasping elm,
think what a pity it will be
when it is gone next year.

BEHIND THE BARN ON GRADUATION DAY
(Grandpa Hank)

We were all there—almost as many
as at the State Championship.
Kids between our legs.
Lynnette, all grown up, near the edge;
even that strange Barr woman
who custom farms with Leroy was there.

Asa and Phil Green got into it—
grating over Asa's going
to township meetings in two townships.
Asa said he could because his house sits in one,
his grandma's house sits just across the line.
Phil said the only reason he still held on
to the old homestead was to try outfoxing
the bankruptcy court and that was wrong.
We gave both of them Mabel's special punch,
calmed them down.

We talked about things.
Always the same—nothings and everythings—
you know, all those daily things: rain, seed,
latest purchases, animals and weeds.
Walt recollected as he had never
seen such contrary weather:
so dry early, since then the skies weep
as if they sat at a dozen funerals.
Someone called it Mother Nature's mean streak:
a trick so seed comes different each year—
this time good for beans, hard on corn.
Next year both gasping for life
while oats yield tons in heads, if not dollars.

I say "wonder when the next drought
will hit?" and for a moment there is nothing
but the sound of kids...
it's hard to fight a lack of water.

We joked, our voices bouncing off the faded red wall.
Mildred heard us, thought we were too rowdy.
She told us to come back to the house;
it was time to serve the cake.

KYLE GRADUATES (Jo)

No time to think what it all means.
Too much cleaning, painting and replacing to do.
I threw out half the games in the closet,
snatched away old tennis shoes.

Foolish woman—
I called in carpenters
to fix the dining room window
a month before the party.
The invitations for 100 went out the same day.

They should have finished it in an afternoon.
They covered the hole with a sheet,
promised to come back.
It stormed the next three nights.

The wind drove rain through the cotton,
blotched the floor. At 2:00 a.m.
I covered it with what was on hand—
plastic wrap. Jake hooted when
he woke up and saw it. He threw an arm
across my shoulders, laughing so hard
I had to smile, too, though my eyes were wet.

Next day I called the floor people.

The room was finally ready
three days before baccalaureate.

Kyle heard from aviation school—
his father doesn't know yet.
Still no chance to think things slowly.
We rolled on "to do" lists
right through to today.

Now people pour across my freshly
finished floor. They look through
my new window and ask Kyle
the same questions—
where he goes and when.
The coffee flows.
Then, suddenly, it is late.
The last couple leaves.

Kyle looks around at the dishes,
empty cups, and comes to me.
We hug.

There is a moment sometimes,
when you touch your child—
something electric passes through you both.
Maybe it is ghosts whirling by.
For a moment time and place are just right.
He steps away and goes out grinning.

Lynnette and I clean up,
stack plates that Jake carries in.
Kyle pulls down the paper lanterns
on the patio.

We don't talk much; not about the diploma
resting on the desk, not about what is next.
Our thoughts hang in the June air,
heavy as the sun which cannot
bear to stay up any longer.

JOHN DEERE $93,000.00 SALE (Mabel Prangle)

Here we go again.
He never passes this place.

Even when he intends to go by,
at the last minute he whips the old truck in,
shakes up to the display room.

It is come
so I hate to return
those sales boys' smiles,
happy to see us.

I stay in the cab
while they crowd around
the biggest, newest model.
He never looks my way.
He doesn't care how hot it gets.

For twenty-four years he has said
'no' to new curtains. I wash all those dishes
in my old kitchen, with a sink jammed into
a pantry out-of-date half a century ago.
He won't replace the leaky toilet tank,
or lift the rotting floor boards.

He says the farm account
can't handle it right now.

Every year it happens.
Those John Deere boys hand him
glossy brochures.

He rubs his chin,
plays with his calculator.
Then he hauls over last year's model,
trades it in, and he buys.

Oh, what he buys!
Always on sale, of course.

STILL AHEAD: THE REST OF JULY AND ALL OF AUGUST

Slow and firm,
        firm and slow
                comes the rain
as if it had always been there;
as if it should not have come six weeks ago,
                or more.

Firm and slow
      ignoring its absence
the way the cat ignores the sudden gap in her litter.

Slow and firm
 the earth takes the rain
as if it never needed it,
as if it has not blown tears of dust for days.

Birds whose voices have not pierced
the withdrawing green
for over two dozen sunsets
sing as if they never knew a silence.

Hard and dry
    we are still drought-wrapped.
Parched islands,
we cannot celebrate with wild dancing
when all around us remain unmoved
about their own death and life.

Firm and slow
        the rain disdains our need for violence.
              It slides down, as if turning the calendar page.
     As if to whither our expectations it comes,
            slow and firm.

GAMBLING WITH JULY (Jo and Jake)

Each year we play the game.
We start in April,
tense until the fields dry and finally open.
We bounce higher than the spring day,
stretch the hours between sunrise and sundown.

Next, the peace of June.
Heat shimmers off the furrows
between thunderstorm soakers.
Our hopes are as bright as the rainbow.

July comes in to oppress us,
      no compromises.
Our expectations shrivel;
corn-promises curl up in one oven-afternoon.

Each year we play the game,
panting for relief.

Everything fuels the heat:
a mailbox with only bills,
doing without for one more week,
never knowing if times will get better.

Each year we lay on sheets at night,
feet burning,
windows open to catch
any hoarse scratch of wind.
We turn,
left,   right,
    around again,
unable to sleep,
there is a stale taste of defeat
on the back of our tongues.

We try to ignore what
the stars whisper and the moon repeats—
but here it comes again.
They ask: is this your last year?
Once more we roll the dice.

PRESERVING THE MOMENT

They are all in this picture,
awkwardly suspended.
They must have asked someone
who doesn't like cameras to snap it—
Bill perhaps, or Asa when he came over for coffee.

Lynnette does not look pretty:
her skin unusually yellow,
her lithe figure slumped low
on her chair.

Kyle's flight jacket hangs askew.

Grandma's hand wanders
near Grandpa's shirttail.
He stands above Jake
hand hard on Jake's shoulder
as if to anchor him in place.

Only Jo, face dimpled,
looks serene and composed,
but less than an hour earlier
she had learned of her Gran McGregor's death—
gone, last link to her family.

The photo frame is crooked,
even less perfect than the subjects.

It is tucked between Kyle's senior shot,
Jake and Jo's greening wedding pose
on the dusty mantle top.

But which of them would throw it away?
It is, after all, the whole Carlson family.

THE WAY OF CRICKETS

Night walk.
No change in cricket's tenor
when boots crunch
or dog barks.
They eat the dark,
sound constant as summer.
They ignore lightning flash
on southern ridge.
When the wind shifts
their chant never modulates,
always remains three paces
behind, never closer,
never warm,
never individual.

Act Two: Turns

WATCHING THE NEST (Jo)

This dark house is mine.
I am free to wander
without day disturbances.
I possess any room I choose.
Tonight I move to the hallway,
halfway between my sleeping children.
The yard light sifts into the room
through the window.
Again I watch them sleep.

Years ago I would breathe with Kyle and Lynnette.
It seemed their baby air was rough,
mine anxiety jagged. Yet they slept on.
As time widened I listened
to my boy murmur his day.
Sometimes he would giggle out loud.

When young they begged me to stay.
I stood here and sang of moon or winds
that laughed half the summer night.
They tried to stay awake.
Their eyes would open 7, 8, 9 times,
then shut. They sighed.
I was there.

They turned all arms and legs,
impossibly skinny.
Their trunks flung out across
beds suddenly too short.
Tonight, they are nearly man and woman.
I have always night watched them.

Last year in the daylight I went to
their rooms, searched for something to remark on
in case some night they stirred and found me there.
I thought I could comment casually
"Oh see, I was passing by—look how your shade hangs..."

One night it happened.
Lynnette opened her eyes,
moonlight on skin and hair.
I blurted "I was watching
how beautiful your body is."
She stretched and smiled.
"I love you, too, mom."

Now Kyle is leaving.
He will only return for quick
breaks filled with his friends.
Lynnette begins her last year at home.
These rooms will soon be
silent as the stars passing above.

I have years of barefoot crossings
over this old wood floor.
I have counted snowflakes pulsing under the yard light,
moved from the rich smell of spring growing
to fall shaking loose.
I kept them safe with my vigils.

After they leave I will not know when they cry out,
I will move in the dark alone.

I DO NOT MIND (Kyle)

Lynnette and I fought one time,
when I told her I didn't love
the land here. She kicked me.
I don't know what made her so angry.

Mom works hard to decorate
the rooms and make each holiday special.
I try to tell her thanks, I know
she wants my appreciation

I like the house and yard just fine.
I know I can come back any time,
ease it around my shoulders,
ward off any homesickness.

But this place doesn't hold me.
Soil is just soil.
The garden is blooming.
I am glad it will still be here.
I just don't want to help keep it.

I don't see myself taking
Dad's truck back to town,
I can't see months of checking grain bins.
I don't see myself cutting the field open
as if I owned it.

When you are in the sky you can see
no-one possesses the land.
Mom, Lynnette, sorry,
but I am opening my arms wide
and running right for the cliff
so I can glide away;
air my only possession,
your ground far below me.

FAMILY FARM CHANGES (Jake)

He told me he is leaving.
Even before today
I felt his restlessness.
I thought he might go—
not just to listen to schools
or bring back new ideas—
just go.

He told me he was going.

We were walking the beans,
checking damage
from ice balls which last night
battered against my encouragement.
The earth gave up
fresh cold of thunder rain.

I touched the bean leaf,
tattered,
assessed the loss.

He wants to take up the city
as if he felt at home with
concrete and walls.
He will settle in with faces
as if they were better
than corn rows.

He told me he is going.
I listened.

What more is there to say?

ON THE VERGE (Jo)

The view from the plunging plane:
window reveals clouds roaring up,
ground presses greener.
The mind must slow,
an oasis of calm,
while the heart beats fear.
Nothing can be done,
just pray the pilot
pulls up before down takes over.

Gran McGregor must have felt such a plunge:
heart wild, cold mind analyzing the dust
that smothered their bank account.
Her countdown until the sheriff's horse
turned up the drive. The closed door.
One sad look at jade fields
filled with repossessed.

The reporters try to catch
the passengers' changes.
Survivors shake heads,
hold their hands to face
as if to keep their soul inside.

Gran's changes were there, too—
crevices around her eyes,
the sharp crack in her voice.

Each day I face the mirror.
Mind calm, I watch.
I am looking to see if
my face etches like Gran's did.
I lean close, checking.
After each new plunge—
the bank demanding additional collateral,
the rain, two weeks late,
the rise in the cost of feed—
I search my own reflection.

PLANTING TIME (Jake)

The green was slow this spring,
as slow as the medics
after Pop halted in the yard,
wavered forward
one step,
two.

He fell, dirt puffing around him.
Steel clouds hovered
and for the first time
it smelled like rain.

I was with Pop when they finally
lifted him into the red flash of life.
I saw his arm rigid,
his face greyer than my cow
at slaughtering time.

He was breathing, then.

THE RISE AND FALL (Grandma Mildred)

I watched him drop.
The bread was just punched,
I was kneading.
He jolted,
moved as if in a dream,
then tumbled down.
My hands kept working the dough
while I tried to understand what I saw.
I finally shook it off when I saw Jake's face
as he ran across the yard to him.

I grabbed my towel,
wiping my hands as I went to them.
Jake pushed me back saying "call for help"
and my feet turned around towards my screen door.
I could see them through it as I dialed.

The sun poured over the yard.
The smell of yeast touched me.
Sirens, faint and warning,
moved from town towards our place.

NORTHERN COMFORT (Asa Prangle)

When you hear sirens
it hurts to look across your field—
you know it will touch you, somehow.
I grabbed my hat, hollered to Mabel.
We hoisted up into my '65 Chevy,
followed the sound down the highway.
It was the Carlson's.
Hank was down.

Jake and his mother,
fuzzy and afraid,
talked about calling folks.
I said I'd handle it. Jake nodded
from the back of the ambulance,
I'm not sure he even heard me.

After we called Jo and the kids,
Bill and I cleaned up the yard.
We worked with the cattle
(he never could have managed alone).
The rotor-tiller stood in the garden
so I gave it a few spins.
Still two good hours of daylight left.
Mabel had bread baking,
the warm smell beckoned in the yard.
She cleared away kitchen things,
put up a big casserole,
wrapped tight in the back of the fridge.

I was fifteen when the neighbors
came to my family,
helped us grieve daddy's death.
Our reaper stood in the corn.
One Saturday twenty neighbors came
to finish up our harvest.
In the middle of the crowded parlor
Mama bent down to me, whispered
"never forget their faces, never."

The Carlsons' cattle are good stock.
I pat their flanks.
It is easy to put coffee on,
bring things in from the garden.
These are such little things.

THE RACE (Lynnette)

Grandpa is even more against
my farming than Dad.
He growls when I ride the tractor.

One time he grabbed me
by the arm, pinched tight,
snarled I was 'not enough
help to my grandmother;
worried my mother too much—
what made me think
I could do any good acting like a man?'—
he talked and talked.
I tried to be a stone but a tear slid out.
My stomach hurt, too.

He stretches out in this white bed,
surrounded by medicine smells.
A machine beeps each time
he makes an uneven sigh.
I try not to think about
what he said that day.
My stomach flips.

Grandma is near.
I touch her cheek,
but she never looks up.
Dad sits.
He rubs one hand over the other
until I reach out, stop them
with my own hand.

I hate the thought
racing around my head.
My stomach flips,
almost like when we won the school tournament.
I cannot stop it:
my thoughts swoop up and down around the room,
whisper in my ear, sink into my body.
"Now I can do more farming."
Although I try not to,
inside, I smile.

TO TAKE TO HEART (Grandpa Hank)

I never knew I was alive
until they jammed those tubes
into me. I could feel my heart.
I finally figured out the need to breathe.

Just at the moment my old body laid down
my mind became so aware.
Lynnette stands by the door,
her skin as smooth as a pearly corn kernel.
I never noticed before.

These tubes block my tongue.
Every motion in the room
brings a separate pain.
I want to call out—
"I am alive.
Let me keep feeling.
I am alive."

DOWN THE HALL (Jo)

Mother Carlson was not
in his room when I came.

She sits in the lounge,
stares out the window,
focuses on the oak tree
just past the parking lot.

She moves as I click near,
touches my skirt.
"Nice suit, Jo, the color sets off your eyes."

We sit and she unravels
the morning slowly,
faltering over the ride in…
"I always dreamt about it, you see."

I nod slowly, my own nightmares sliding
around the edge of my vision.
She squeezes my hand.
"You take good care of Jake."

I don't know if she is warning me,
or finally giving the compliment
I ceased looking for years back.

IN THE ROOM (Jake)

The fan above hums
like wind through the cottonwoods.
The sun warms the blue in my shirt,
but when I lean against the glass it's cool.

I make the arguments for both of us:
"I should have seen it coming;
stopped you lifting heavy bags,
kept you out of the heat."

The nurse rustles in,
smiles without seeing me,
attaches a new bottle.
"He is much better now" she tells
the empty space next to me.
Her mouth curves up, down again,
then she is gone.

I almost hear your argument back:
"I don't like rocking chairs,
could be all my hard work
kept this day away
one extra heartbeat."

You are still,
tongue frozen by tubes.
I think of all the silences
that have run between us before.

THE DOCTOR'S PRESCRIPTION

The house may be too big for you now.
No lifting.
No strenuous chores
    in chilly spring sunrise
    or humming August afternoons.
Stay out of the heat, and don't stand in rain.
No ratcheting around in heavy equipment,
face plastered with bean dust.
Avoid snatches of hot coffee,
        mouthfuls of lukewarm sandwiches.
No five a.m. eggs,
        no fresh cinnamon rolls at ten.
Stay away from beef,
        eat less at suppertime.
Let others do those chores.

You should think about moving to town.

ACT THREE: HARVEST

NEARING CULMINATION (Jake)

There is only flame bush color
where the sun was.
High above us the moon is a breast,
    nipple bright,
fullness hidden in blue shadow.
We porch-sit,
listen to night sing.
The crickets chant "harvest."
All plants hold their breath.
The earth smells moist.

Jo sits close.
Her lips are wet
from sips of sweet plum wine.
There is a new depth to her eyes,
a thick swing to her hair.

We feel the sharper wind,
short summer already slipping
around the corner of September.
I know it is almost time.

Almost.

One week, maybe two—
until the crickets are just the right tenor,
until the air will wait no more—
then we can gather up summer.
Then we can look to winter bed.

It is almost time—
almost.

In the dark I reach out,
stroke her cool skin.

THE PRODUCT OF LABOR (Jake and Lynnette)

The wild green dance
has left these beans.
They cool to a yellow waltz
in the span from Monday to Friday.
Each day they brown further,
leaves pulling into themselves,
until they hunch
in a fetal hug
at center stage.

As they slow,
our own cotillion builds.
In yard and road we shift discs,
tune up combines, hone blades.

Our pulse keeps tempo,
we tap our toes as we gather.
The crops stand still:
corn with lowered heads,
soybeans heavy.
The engines rumble
a prelude across the section.
Even the sun trembles
with expectation.
We climb the tractor,
ready to start.

PREDAWN RITUAL (Jo)

The room is a shadow of last night.
I turn, deep under the blankets,
reach, and find nothing.

Jake is already up.
The clink of a glass from the bathroom.
My one eye reluctantly pulls open,
seeks the clock: 5:00 a.m.

He comes across the room.
I stretch towards his arms,
"It is an hour before the alarm.
Come back to bed. Stay."

"I can't.
The cattle truck will be
at Pop's in 20 minutes."
He sits on the bed,
leans over to kiss me,
pulls up my warmth,
inhales my sleepiness.
"I wish I could. I want to stay."

Then there is only
the dip where he sat.
The sunrise intrudes as
the pickup pulls out of the drive.

Outside my window
the mourning dove
predicts her departure
from the big oak.

FULL CIRCLE (Jo)

He is in the fields.
He starts in black:
quick movement
from his side of the bed,
coffee smell from below.
Eye blinks later I stir again.
In the grey I hear his tractor
two fields past the house.

I clean dishes,
sweep the floor,
move school things and mail.
I know everything will stay
the same until I come home again.

At twilight on the gravel road
I see the dust of our cornstalk chopper,
wonder who is driving it.
I work on dinner,
pack a bucket for Lynnette
to take to him.

I sit at the kitchen table
to pay bills.
The sun goes down.
One combine still moves
through corn rows.
The bean field lies empty.

At ten I stand by the door,
strain to see how much is left—
go to bed.
Later he comes in,
hat thumping against his knee.
I sneeze awake.

We talk as he showers,
steam filling the room.
"Beans at sixty-five bushels an acre!
Sixty-five!"
We out-laugh the water.

ACT THREE: HARVEST

He cannot wait for day
to start again.
The north wind and scudding clouds
make him frantic.

"Winter will be better," he groans
as the bed jounces, "full of snow days,
fires and quiet talks."

He snores,
mutters "sixty-five"
throughout the short night.

AFTERMATH OF CORN HARVEST (Jo)

For a breath you do not
comprehend the alteration.
Your eyes sweep across the night,
hesitate.

You linger on stark white
not there the evening before.

The corn is gone.
The night has changed.

Summer's close warmth
bows to hard spots of yard lights.

For a breath you pause,
puzzled.
Your eyes stretch to horizons
not seen since spring.

You sense the town,
distant and aloof.

Somehow,
to see so far
makes the dark colder.

FINISHING TOUCHES (Jake)

The combine goes back to the yard.
All the stalks have been chopped,
the last furrow rolled over.
On the edge of the bean field
the bare cottonwoods sigh.

The corn piled high near the bins
is the only sunshine in the yard.
The ground rests.
The bins digest their contents.
It smells of winter.

I move inside to assess the year.
Sometimes I stare out at my black rows,
watch them stiffen with
each north wind gust.
There is a hiss as the clouds open
and sleep drifts to the ground.

VACATION FROM AG. SCHOOL (Lynnette)

I love this old road.
It winds around these hills
like mid-morning coffee talk.
My tires sing
"home for Christmas."

For the first time
since finals, I relax.
Snow lies as a welcome mat
across my familiar fields.
Each neighbor's house
is gift wrapped.

Now I turn the corner—
last county road before the gravel.
I am almost home.
Dad will look at the brochures I bring,
we can talk about the newest techniques.

Mom and I will edge around Robert Rodriguez
the boy in my biology lab.
Maybe I will tell her what Rob said—
he wants an equal partner on his farm.

Next week I pick up Kyle at the airport.
We will speak about roommates,
laugh over old family jokes.

On Christmas Eve we'll go to Grandma's
to sing carols. Grandpa will toast us
with her eggnog, if the doctor lets him.
On Christmas, we'll unwrap love all day.

Tonight the cold stings my car window,
but it can't touch my warmth.
I twinkle back at the flakes
dancing in my headlights.

This is my holiday, today, next year.
My future is just around the curve.

A LOW OKLAHOMA HOOKER (Grandma Mildred)

Your side of the bed is dark.
Your breath catches.
I wait, holding my own breath.
I live with the fear that each
noise you make means we shall
repeat yet again the sudden seizures.

I feel the sameness
of all the changes—
how you grow slower still,
how your fingers fumble.
That spunk of yours,
which kept me with you
all these years, is slipping, too.

I wish we had gone to town.
I shake my head.
So weak when it comes
to you. Your last two strokes
might not have hit so hard
if we had a quiet house
on some little street.

You gargle.
Outside thunder replies.
It is disturbing--
thunder in December.
Snow pelts against the window.
These things do not belong
together, but here they are,
as if taunting me—
saying this will be
what life is from here on in.

I am tired.

So weary of the feedings,
the slow drag across the room;
hefting you to the bathroom stool.

You are as angry as thunder in a blizzard.

Each time you stuggle I lose a little more
of the bit of me that was left.

I am tired.

Christmas makes me cry.
I don't want the lights;
children's voices;
even my baking, which used
to mean so much, goes flat.

This wind pushes against me
until I want to shove back.
It questions all I have done—
I have no answers.

The window rattles.
Suddenly, I wish I could
tell these things to Jo.
She and I held things so differently.

The wind hisses at me tonight, taunts
that she is right and I was always wrong.

I am too tired to fight the low thunder.
I close my eyes.
Good bye, Hank.

ACT THREE: HARVEST

AFTER THE BLIZZARD (Bill)

It seems you can't keep
death out of some days.
It creeps up like a December sun
after a big storm,
pale but taking over cold dawn.

I had just come from the barnyard
to tell them about the frozen calf
when I saw Mr. Carlson.
He was leaning against
the door in his night shirt,
his stick trembling at his side,
his other hand limp by the doorknob.
He winced in the glare,
rose a shaky arm to point at me.

I waded through the deep snow,
pushed the door open,
helped him to a chair.
He turned his watery eyes
towards the other room,
words dribbling against
his chin uselessly.

I went, saw her there.
I spread the sheet and made him coffee.
After the phone call we sat,
my hand over his,
waiting for the plows to go by.

Much later, after the house emptied,
I picked up the phone and dialed Ma.

In the gold slant of the sunset
we talked of the five years
come between us
since last I went back
to her little place in town.

STAVING OFF GHOSTS (Jo)

Father left me when I was seven
after countless leavings; times
filled with shouts, a slammed door,
empty bottles rolling across the kitchen.
Mother, swollen and moving slowly
muttered "It does not matter."
She never said his name again.

We moved in with Gran McGregor.
Every Christmas Eve I sat,
my nose burning on the frosted window.
I wished for him to come on stars,
snowflakes, even the shimmering tree.
After too many Christmases
I echoed my mother. "It does not matter."

Mother left when I turned fifteen.
Cancer gnawed at her until I couldn't bear
to kiss the dip that had been her cheek.
It blew so cold I thought the flowers
would shatter when they fell.
It did not matter.

My brother left just as he turned eighteen.
While hunting he walked like Jesus
out a quarter of a mile on November ice
of Laura Lake. He hung on for twenty minutes.
For two days I was silent. What did it matter?

Gran and I went on alone. Her sight failed,
she sometimes called me my mother's name.
My wedding cost her the next nine days in bed.
She faded out while Kyle was still flying toy airplanes.

I shook off my ghosts, became the perfect wife.
My children knew only a happy mother.
Now Grandma Carlson lies in the mortuary.
We stand in the dark corner of her room.
One time I think I hear her whisper,
I reply before I can stop myself.

My daughter weeps.
I whisper "It does matter."

ACT THREE: HARVEST

MAKING DO (Jake)

The guys at the Co-op
tell how it just doesn't pay
to the let the heart take over
in these matters. False charity,
they say. It drains the pocket book
to keep feeding a dried up cow.

I make things work.
My old dog is so deaf
she doesn't bark when
the neighbor's pickup pulls in.
There's no room for charity,
they say.
I nod again,
load Rex's 50 lb bag.

Their wives touch my sleeve,
say they are sorry to hear about
Mother's death, just too much
after Pop's stroke;
they tell how nice Shady Lane Home is.
I smile thanks, make sure to
drop off my letter to Meals on Wheels.

The home-care nurse is all arranged.
Our hired hand Bill moves his things
to the main house tomorrow.

The Carlsons have fed old cows,
blind cats and deaf dogs
for over one century.
We do just fine showing such charity.
I have a lot of years ahead of me.
I will make this work.

JANUARY PROGRESS (Jake)

The work is all still here,
even when sun dogs
hang in an ice sky.
Cattle still need grain
forced down from bins.
The yard steams with their life.

Beyond them my fields are empty.

The air has no smell.
Each day twilight runs so short
the black beats you to evening feedings.

I am still in winter.
All the work is here, but without
the sound of trees, it is more of a struggle.

Now the computer rustles for me
until the leaves can come back.
The radio in the corner
counts off more than futures,
it tells me a Chinook will soon
shake loose, take me back
into my living cycles.

Jo says I need this frozen time.
I have to breathe cautiously
so my lungs will not shatter.
From my office window the ever
present wind wisps snow into
north-south arrows,
pointing to my untouchable fields.

I am Spring, a planting tenor.
I am sun and wind.
I break down the winter,
so it remembers how to move time.

Watch for me when the redwing
returns on the first spring sunrise;
I'll be outside, tasting the dirt.

ACKNOWLEDGEMENTS

The following poems were previously published

Aftermath of Corn Harvest	The Moccasin 2000
Biding Time	The Best of Northlight 1990
Bill The Farm Hand	County Lines, Loonfeather Press, 2008
Cage From Within	The Best of Northlight 1990
Hayloft's Gift of Night	Crossings, Poet-Artist Collaboration, 2015;
	The Best of Northlight 1990
Finishing Touches	The Moccasin 2002
Love in Planting Season	The Moccasin 1992;
	The Best of Northlight 1990
Still Ahead:	
The Rest of July and All of August	Southwest Journal, 1992
The Product of Labor	The Moccasin 2001
The Way of Crickets	MnArtists (mnartists.org) 2008
	The Moccasin 2002
When Things Are Good	The Best of Northlight 1990
Windshield Window Peeping	The Moccasin 2000

Work on this manuscript was supported by a 2014 grant from the McKnight Foundation for Emerging Artists received through Prairie Lakes Regional Arts Council, Inc. in Minnesota. I am especially grateful to John Rezmerski for his challenging, insightful and creative suggestions that made this manuscript come together.

Finally, I want to thank those closest to me. I was supported by the love and encouragement of my husband, Henry Panowitsch, and family members (all fellow poets) Christina Flaugher and Colin Chambers whose comments and support helped me make this dream a reality.

Front Cover Photo: Chip Borkenhagen
Back Cover Photo: John Cross

About the Author
Susan Chambers

Susan was a practicing attorney for over 34 years and now serves as the Blue Earth County Court Referee, a judicial position. She has written throughout that time. Among Susan's literary publications are some unusual venues: Minneapolis Regional News; UU Minister's Publication; Minn. Law and Politics Magazine; Family Law Forum-a magazine for divorce attorneys; The Legal Studies Forum "Off the Record, an Anthology of Poetry by Lawyers".

She won the National Federation of State Poetry Society's Grand Prize ($1,000.00 and $1,500) on two separate occasions (NFSPS "Encore"). She is published in numerous anthologies: County Lines-Loonfeather Press; Moccasin-League of Minnesota Poets; Encore(multiple years); Pasque Petals-South Dakota State Poetry Society; The Best of Northlight Writers Conference and the on-line publication "Write on". She was a winner for three years running in the MnLIT competitions..

Susan has presented poetry workshops in schools in Minnesota, Texas, Utah and Iowa. She has presented poetry, copyright and publishing contract speeches in Louisiana, Arkansas, Indiana, Iowa, Utah, Florida, Minnesota, South Dakota and Wisconsin. She does presentations at churches, Kiwanis, senior citizen and civic and poetry groups. She does poetry performances statewide at coffee houses, art galleries and just about anywhere someone wants to hear poetry. Susan resides on a country acreage in Blue Earth County, with her husband Henry and one old cat.